In Your Absence

Jill Penny

smith|doorstop

the poetry business

Published 2021 by
Smith|Doorstop Books
The Poetry Business
Campo House,
54 Campo Lane,
Sheffield S1 2EG

ISBN 978-1-912196-42-5
Typeset by The Poetry Business
Printed by People for Print

Smith|Doorstop Books are a member of Inpress:
www.inpressbooks.co.uk

Distributed by NBN International, 1 Deltic Avenue,
Rooksley, Milton Keynes MK13 8LD

The Poetry Business gratefully acknowledges the support of
Arts Council England.

Contents

for Jack and Lily with love

Part One

Blunt Force Trauma

Today, this hour, this minute, there are things I need
to be true, and to not be true.
I need it to be true that on that night it really was help offered,
by that young lad, not the broken ribs from three to twelve,
shattered cheek bones, both eye sockets broken,
smashed nose and the fractured skull
resulting from a blunt force trauma.

I need it to be true that in the intimacy of a pocket,
hands were searching for your phone to call for help,
or at the very least feeling the quality of your suit,
which looked expensive, looked like privilege,
which was second hand.
That the lad was *only asking for the time*
and that I never knew the meaning of a contrecoup.

I need it to not be true, that there are people who have *nothing*,
have not got a lot, that rumour had it was some Asian lad.
True, that he was *looking for a job to get his life on track*.
Not true, the lifelong trauma, the blunt force of 'care.'
True a lad like him could save himself from life,
from dealing and enduring further blows. And most, I need it to be true,
that when you told the paramedics you were fine

that you were fine.

Things I See on the Hard Shoulder

In the days before our wild and precious lives
began to choke us before the brain bleed and the ventilator tube
I spend 50 days and nights in search of you between Manchester and Leeds
Distraught and terrified owned by the road I am the pulse
of the windscreen wipers and the flare of lights on the westbound carriageway
dangerously distracted by the things I see on the hard shoulder

1. Shreds of sheeting grey as your skin whip-torn, forlorn, a vast ghost flapping down the whole sad length of the M62
2. A never-ending diesel slipstream
3. A hard hat, white, rolling like a skull
4. An oily rainbow a parallel universe a dark holding place a reverse film on slippery celluloid we are the flickering ones streaming past each other frame after frame

and three animals
I saw them love *lying between us*

5. Grit coloured cat, sex unknown, moments before brutally kicked back by tyres still kicking back

3 seconds

6. Red dog fox, solid, heavy busted bag of bone and blood, his back to three lane brush blasted by wind rush

3 seconds

7. Roe deer. Female. Rigid with fear. Eyes in headlights blue. The blue and blinding howl of a siren

3 seconds 3 seconds 3 seconds

In Your Absence

Hospital

Woman

I smoke cigarettes, in the kitchen,
every night, waiting for the phone to ring.
Counting makes me feel that I am
in control when I am not.

Daughter

Example: Heartbeat of windscreen wipers as we hurtle between London, Manchester and Leeds almost daily.

Example: Steps. Sixty. Leading up onto the ward. We never take the lift.

Example: Doors. Five. Lined up along the corridor before we reach the door where your whispered name into the intercom admits us to the semi darkness of the ICU like a spell.

Man

Example: Breath.

Woman

There is a suitcase where you were sitting yesterday
I experience extreme synaesthesia as you lie there in a nylon gown
I have to leave when you cannot.

Daughter

Sound of respirator smell of disinfectant barely concealing fear

House

Woman

I place clothes and books and coffee in the suitcase
where you were sitting only yesterday
Someone has put white blinds up in the house
where you were living up until last year
there will be an anniversary soon and in your absence
this year will have rolled on by despite my stumbling in its path.

Something haunts me
It is white, as in, the whites of your rolling eyes, as in your

Man

White Lies / Feather / Magic

Man and Daughter

Bone White / Water / Wedding

Daughter

Blood Cells / Hope / White Light

Woman and Daughter

Noise

Daughter

There are three new photographs around the house

Woman

I move them into different rooms and into drawers and out again
You are monochrome
You are drinking in New York wearing my vintage dress
You are absent

Daughter

Body fading

Dream I

Woman

The first white number according to the rules for colouring numbers is 66. I find this significant in ways I can't explain. Finding myself lost in colour, especially the number blue, I wrap my arms in your abandoned sheets and fall asleep before it gets dark.

Daughter

Dream poem

Woman

You kissed me in the blue lit public toilets
You were passionate as never so in life
You were eating peas out of the bird feeder
I said that was unhygienic.

Man

Irrelevant

Woman

It was always summer in the public toilet
There was a mirror made of tin

Man

It was winter outside in the garden
White out

Woman

I couldn't see you. You began to cry. A tear ran down your cheek onto the pillow.
You were my neighbour in the garden

Daughter

Then you weren't.

Woman

Why do you come kissing me?
It isn't like you
Are you making up for lost lost time?

Dream II

Daughter

My brother and I
sway together laughing
underwater
in our sandy beach shoes
in the sweet piss smelling
blue lit public toilet

Buckets emptied of our catch of crabs
left outside with needles cones and scent of pines.
We're walking home with Mum and Dad
trailing metal spades along
Beach Road for our tea
because it's five o'clock.

My mother roughly tugs
my little swimming costume
down revealing strap marks.
White against the red. The angry sting
of sunburnt shoulders makes me howl.

As your absence hurts and makes me howl
and is outrageous to me.

Garden

Woman

Before I realised it, I was in the throes of an obsession. I spent my time, in your absence, reflecting on the fact that the colour or non-colour white reflects and scatters powerful wavelengths of light, and that I experience these wavelengths physically, in the presence of all things white.

In the darkening days of October, continually craving this sensation and this stimulation I planted lily of the valley, yarrow, elder, jasmine, nettles, snowdrops for the spring.

Daughter

In February there was snow. Some days we chose to see the snow as one. Some days we sat for hours at the window counting snowflakes, hailstone and each frosted blade of grass before the thaw and then at last the snowdrops.

Woman

White is nothing but a startling absence, although in my experience, is the opposite of absence. I know what absence looks like. And it is not white. It is not innocent or pure or safe.
It is however true that white stains easily, that all things are mutable.

Daughter

Example: Blossom from the cherry tree in April is abundant, annual, short-lived.

Example: One foxglove, white, grows from the same place in the dry stone wall, biannually.

Man

Example: The plaster cherub with one arm, the Buddah and the chalk face in the garden crumble quietly into heaps of dust, a little more decrepit every year.

Woman

Other white things I spend my time considering are ashes in the fire pit reminiscent of another scattering of ashes, fake pearls clinging to a dress, cocaine, lies. More lies. A tribe of cats, blank pages in a note-book, feathers flying from a slit pillow.

Mother

The clouds in my eyes

House

Woman

Immersion in the colour or non-colour white aids mental clarity, so in the bright days of July, craving this sensation and this stimulation I painted every single room in our house white and hung white curtains for my birthday. I keep them closed all day and watch the shadow play of birds and ivy from my bed.

Daughter

It's not ok

Woman

There are hundreds of rooms in our house. Most are accessible only through the dream door. Awake and up all night I stare into the bathroom mirror, and then into the white spare room where you ended up before the whole thing ended. Up into the empty attic with the dizzying drop and bed our children were conceived in. Down into the living room with its garden doors, our stained glass windows bringing colour to the white walls. I think about us bringing the piano home in a horse box. It's where I stand most nights, leaning on it, as I would a friend, looking back into the empty rooms.

Daughter

I can't stay here.

Hospital

Man

It's a white-knuckle ride!

Daughter

Quiet voice of consultant calm authoritative barely concealing pity

Man

Don't shoot till you can see the whites of their eyes!

Daughter

Body fading

Man

Ladies and gentlemen, boys and girls let me introduce to you THE DNR! (Do Not Resuscitate, cheeky!) And next for your delight, THE MORPHINE DRIVER followed by REMOVAL OF THE LIFE SUPPORT and almost last of all THE POST MORTEM, THE REPATRIATION OF THE BRAIN and THE CPS (Crown Prosecution Service to you Madam!) And then THE MOMENT YOU HAVE ALL BEEN WAITING FOR … THE FUNERAL!!!! Scream. Scream if you want to go faster …

Woman

Some nights I wake up screaming.

Garden

Woman

In August we made a wreath with white flowers. Honesty and May blossom. Said to be unlucky if brought into the house.

Daughter

Irrelevant

Woman

I was in London when I got the call

Daughter

I was in London when the news came through

Man

A train pulls out of the railway station. My father in the window waves goodbye

Woman

My mother, never a happy traveller, waiting on the platform, hopes to catch a glimpse of him.

Phone Messages

Mother

Why don't you call me?
They shouldn't leave us all alone like this

Woman

I've been sitting here for hours

Mother

How did you know how to find me here?
You won't be able to find me here.

Daughter

You won't pick up to me. What's wrong with you?

Woman

It's 4am

Man

We are trying to get hold of you from New York

Man and Daughter

Goa Marrakesh

Daughter

Hanoi Berlin

Woman

I am so afraid.
Let's go to Paris

Man

Pick up the bloody phone

Woman

There is a suitcase on the chair where you were sitting yesterday
I experience extreme synaesthesia
You have to leave when I cannot
Sometimes I sleep all day

Dream III

Woman and Daughter

We travelled overnight

Daughter

We took the night train

Woman

Up beyond the Arctic Circle
The temperature read
Minus 30
When we stepped off the train
With rucksacks.
Sturdy boots.
The town snow bound.
Snow piled up in blankets
The station master played 'White Christmas'
On a horn to welcome us
We waited on the wooden platform painted blue
You gathered snowflakes
Big as plates

Daughter

Like the ones you showed me
How to cut from paper once.

Nothing moved at all
We were alone on the wooden platform painted blue
We became elective mutes
Like Hornby figures
In our silent little world
We waited there for hours

Woman

Daylight came and went
There was no difference
Between day and night
I could see the headlights of another train
Kilometres away
But it never reached the station.

Mother

Where are you?
When are you going to come home?
It's getting dark
So early now
They shouldn't leave us all alone like this.

House

Woman

Absence is the opposite of presence. This is the dictionary definition. Absence does not rely on presence just as white does not rely on black but on light. At the height or depth of my obsession, and in your absence, I took up the study of the history of albinism and craved the company of a white peacock. Meanwhile I feasted on nothing other than cauliflower and the hearts of artichoke in November and time rolled back the clock day in day out as you rolled back your eyes and they were white as in

Daughter

White Gold

Man and Daughter

White Heat / Trash

Man

Wood / White Teeth

Mother

Milky White

Daughter

Waking dreaming

Hospital

Woman

Whilst absent from my life I think about America although I have never been there. I am dressed in cocktail black and drinking in The Hamptons, just as you were when the phone call came whilst signing for a suitcase at the hospital, the police station, the lost and found, whilst waiting for the registrar or in the desperate late night café in the hospital I slide reckless into dreams about abandoned buildings. Silent, dark and full of flies and dusty tea lights.

Man

All aboard who's going aboard!

Mother

Are you coming home?

Man

It's the greatest show on Earth THE WALL OF DEATH! For one night only for your entertainment boys and girls, he is riding a wild gurney wearing nothing but a blindfold with his knapsack on his back.

Daughter

You are a bird in flight

Man

Now you see him. Now you don't. And. Now. You. Don't.

Mother

Are you never coming home?

Daughter

You are an astronaut orbiting the Earth in your capsule, on the SS MRI

Woman

You are absent.

These are days that will be marked forever with a white stone in my mind. When the plug was pulled, it became an inevitable act of mutual destruction.

There was the one who never cried and the one who never stopped. Christmas was cancelled. Water circled drains in sinks throughout the hospital, we were not the only ones, and no amount of bleaching could remove the sights the sounds the smells or stop the dirty water backing up so that I had to plunge my hands in it again and again and again.

Garden

Woman

You were gone
before we could repair the rapture
fix the fracture
stem the bleed
assist the breath.

Your absence
lies alone now
swollen in a
hospital gown.
How are you dead?
How are you?
Your presence lingers
on the lane
around the piano
behind the silent sewing machine

through each season
of this terrible year
in the white flowers
and objects I reflect on
in my garden.

How can you not be here
in this wild white abstraction?

House

Daughter

Sparrow in the chimney tumbles into unlit wood stove. Taps on glass. Windows flung wide open. White curtains billow into room. Bird released unharmed and white with ash. Watch her as she disappears into the blue. Body fades.

End

Part Two

The Met Office Predicts a Heavy Fall of Snow

There was another funeral
five years ago.

Broad shouldered bearers
young men
from the valley
slipped on black ice.
The coffin lurched
like the stomachs of the mourners
who with one collective indrawn breath
up lifted him
the son
the brother
father

willed the dreadful cargo
through the chapel door.

Anorexical

I know you have been polishing the trees
flinging sparks around all night

now you are shivering in the aisles

your throat a rat trap

Funeral Flowers

In the freezing vestibule
family flowers lie
stunned on corporation tiles

awkward grief tilts
in an ugly vase
keeping up appearances

The Sin Eaters

Our places set.
Two silver knives
two forks
for lychee and veined oysters
beef steak and cod fish
soul cake and salted butter.
Two spoons
deep dished for
glistening consommé
veal shank hen leg
shallow for a medlar jelly.
Two glasses for the wine.
A spicy red.
We are the sin eaters
gluttonous and honey glazed
swallowing the Ortolan
behind our napkins
spitting out the bones
and beak.
This feast is rich and gamey
malodorous corrupt
and sweet. A delicacy
delicately lying
beneath marzipan
and sugar icing
thick as
time.

Thick Time

returning to the moment
whilst hoping against hope
time is the weight and thickness
of my father's felted overcoat
my mother's fur

constructing an invisibility
whilst washing dishes
time is a sonnet un-written
a fault revealed in time
told by an unreliable clock

pleasures of self-deception
whilst sweeping up the broken glass
time tears the heart out rips it up
pushes it back in
tells us to get on with it

whichever page you open there you are
whilst scrambling towards the exit
time presses a thick bandage to the mouth
we start with love
and we should end with love

Dedicated to the memory of
Paul Bell 1960–2018 and Florence Penny 1925–2018

Acknowledgements

'Thick Time' was written in response to an exhibition of the same name by South African multi-media artist William Kentridge. The exhibition was produced between 2003 and 2016 and 'weaves together global histories of revolution, exile and utopian aspirations, exploring how they are shaped by the creative forces of memory and the imagination' (The Whitworth Gallery, Manchester).